WEIGHT
TRAINING
FOR CATS

WEIGHT TRAINING FOR CATS

by Anthony Serafini
illustrated by Paul Meisel

BALLANTINE BOOKS • NEW YORK

Text copyright © 1982 by Anthony Serafini
Illustrations copyright © 1982 by Paul Meisel

All rights reserved under International and Pan-American Copyright
Conventions. Published in the United States by Ballantine Books, a
division of Random House, Inc., New York, and simultaneously in Canada
by Random House of Canada Limited, Toronto, Canada

Library of Congress Catalog Card Number: 82-90460
ISBN: 0-345-30473-X

Manufactured in the United States of America
Designed by Michaelis/Carpelis Design Assoc., Inc.
First Edition: September 1982
10 9 8 7 6 5 4 3 2 1

CONTENTS

I'D LIKE TO
INTRODUCE
MYSELF....

Flex's the name; muscle's the game. Yes, sir, that's it in a mouse ear. But it took a long time to get from there to here.

It all started in the late '50s in Schenectady, NY, in the middle of my kitty adolescence. There I was, a scrawny, timid cat, living in fear that someone would one day see me running from a mouse. I was in Misery City. Then one day Moxie the Muscle Cat made an appearance at our local furball clinic. What form! What power! What rippling acres of taut muscularity! Well, it was enough to fill this young tom's dreams.

Weight training changed my life for good. No one kicked litter in my face anymore. The word spread like wildfire among the mice of Schenectady: Flex the Cat. The sound of my name had them running and squeaking into their mouse holes in terror.

As my body grew in size and strength, I discovered that I could be the cat I was meant to be. It was all within a paw's reach if I was willing to work like a fiend, day and night, week in and week out. It wasn't easy. There were times when I yearned for a catnip break, a catnap, or maybe just a bout with the old scratching post. But when the Iron Bug bites, it bites hard. And was I bitten!

A regular program of weight training will change your life: You'll gain in self confidence. You'll be more attractive to the opposite sex. You'll be free of dog fear, and you'll be making mouse pancakes of our bare-tailed rodent pests. Best of all, you'll be the cat you were meant to be.

One final word of wisdom: No pain, no gain! Now, go for it!

Three Who Dared for Greatness

I'd like to introduce three very special cats.

Killer Kittee

Killer Kittee was born in a wealthy suburb of Chicago with a silver bell around his neck. Destined for greatness as a captain of industry, the Killer astounded his parents and his prep school when he tossed it all aside to worship the metal god. There's been no looking back for Killer. Twice named Mr. Cat Olympia, Killer's famous risqué "You Ain't Seen Nothin' Yet" poster adorns both gyms and ladies' boudoirs.

Mouse Mangler

Born on the docks of Hoboken, the Mouse Mangler grew up on the other side of the tracks. He was small, attractive in a kittenish way, and terribly sensitive. The Mangler sat on the docks watching the Manhattan skyline and reading Kahlil Gibran. Hoboken was no place for a cat with heart.

The Mangler sadly packed up his rubber mouse and headed south to Bayonne. He decided that he would no longer be a victim of the world's cruelty. Soul was not

enough. The Mangler began working out. After his third week of gym work, he saved nearly the entire litter of a penniless street cat from humiliation at the paws of a band of rabid mice.

Thereafter dubbed the Mouse Mangler, he lifted his way to Mr. Cat America in 1976 and then returned to Hoboken in triumph. A regular at Mario's Muscle Market in his home city, Mr. M. has become a star of the cat bodybuilding circuit. His stunning capture of the Mr. Cat Olympia title in 1980 is still talked about.

Tabby Terrific

One thing you've got to give Tabby Terrific: The kid's got heart. Born in Sarasota, Florida (he still calls it "sarsaparilla"), Tabby never lets the fact that he's not very bright stand in his way. Tabby dropped out of grammar school because he kept falling out of his desk and hitting his head. The Tab recognized that he was the only kitty in the class who could lift the desk off his body from a prone position. One small step for Tabby; one small step for cat body building. The rest is history. Or would have been if he hadn't survived the near-fatal fall from the Empire State Building while attempting to perfect his two-paw cat hang.

THE PHILOSOPHY

The Zen of Weight Training

Do you feel tense and irritable? Do you have a cat-fit every time some little thing goes wrong? Has the spring gone out of your paws? Are your relationships falling apart? Do you secretly feel that it wouldn't take much of a cat to fill your collar?

If you can answer "yes" to any of these questions, your life is probably a mess. This is nothing to feel ashamed of; many cats find that the stresses and strains of modern life leaves them unfocused, jittery,and prone to furballs. But there is a solution. I call it the Zen of Weight Training.

The Zen of Weight Training refers to the cat who is mentally and spiritually centered. As he does his cat-rolls he is at once aware of the process and the goal. His whole being is alert to the flex of his paw, the stretch of his muscle, the rippling of his fur. The kitty who allows the worries and concerns of the day to disappear as a fine mist over the bird bath on a sunny morning will find his mind and his muscles at peace. He might even have an out-of-cat-body experience. Some cats have

gotten so "zenned out" by the mysticism of their muscles that they've kissed dogs.

Of course there are dangers lurking for the cosmically conscious kitty who is becoming the cat he was meant to be. You'll face ridicule from friends, relatives, and cat-haters. They may start calling you "Kundalini Kitty" or "Karma Cat." They'll disparage your new joy and machismo. Where once you were a "weakling" now you'll be called "musclebound." You used to be an "emotional disaster area" and now you're "blissed out." It's a no-win situation.

I advise highly sensitive kitties to work out with cats sharing their dedication. There is strength in numbers. Once other cats begin to see your new sense of "self," and the awesome energy you radiate, those doubting felines will be pestering you for tips on their own bodybuilding program. Be patient. Remember, when the Iron Bug bites, he truly bites hard.

Why Weights?

Many kitties marvel at the taut muscularity and obvious boundless power of cats like the Mouse Mangler and myself. They say "Wow, catpower!" and "Flash a flex, you fab felines!" when we pass on the street. They're impressed, no doubt about it. But these kitties never dream that they themselves could sport such muscle boulders on their own bodies. And that's where they're wrong. The mantra for the cat beginning weight training is: Any Kitty Can!

It's true. Any cat can stalk birds with power and precision, flatten mice with dazzling speed, and impale goldfish with pinpoint accuracy. Any cat can have a body to die for. It's all in the weights.

Why Me?

Is weight training the sport for you? This is one question you'll have to answer for yourself. I would like to point out, however, that there are some good reasons to get into weight training and some bad:

The following are GOOD reasons to pump iron:
- To be a sensation on the beach with a mighty cat body
- To save ladycats when they are in danger
- To increase your kitty self-esteem and be the cat you were meant to be

The following are BAD reasons to press pecs:
- To steal food whenever possible from weaker cats
- To beat up on cats who violate your turf
- To get a job as a numbers runner

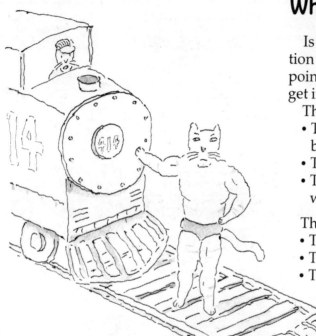

GOOD

The question remains: can you, personally, handle weight training? The following questionnaire will help you examine your spiritual and physical condition.

The Cat Soul

Check one:

I spend most of my day:
- **A.** Cruising for burgers
- **B.** Napping
- **C.** Doing aerobic exercises

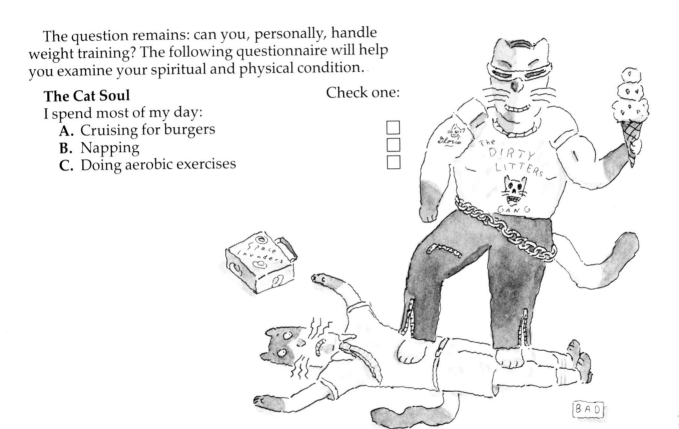

My favorite vacation spot is:
  A. McDonald's ☐
  B. Dairy Queen ☐
  C. The "challenger" slope at Aspen ☐

I like a ladycat who:
  A. Has a knockout figure and dresses
    to prove it ☐
  B. Won't keep calling the next day ☐
  C. Wants me to be the cat I was meant to be ☐

When I'm depressed I:
  A. Call up a friend and argue ☐
  B. Try to blame it all on my parents ☐
  C. Meditate until I'm at peace with myself
    and the rest of the world ☐

I would like to exercise but:
  A. I just ate ☐
  B. I'm too short ☐
  C. There's nothing stopping *me* ☐

You get 10 points for every "C" answer. If your score is less than 50, your spirit could use some shaping up for sure. Now we'll check out the old bod.

The Cat Body

After I nap I:
- **A.** Go back to sleep ☐
- **B.** Find it almost impossible to stand up ☐
- **C.** Often play a set or two of tennis ☐

When I scamper through the woods:
- **A.** My stomach makes footprints ☐
- **B.** I collapse after three yards and call a cab ☐
- **C.** I feel exhilarated and glad to be alive ☐

Five sit ups:
- **A.** Would kill me ☐
- **B.** Is my favorite punk rock group ☐
- **C.** Would just get me warmed up ☐

At the beach:
- **A.** I'm often mistaken for a sand dune ☐
- **B.** I wear a "cover-up" even when swimming ☐
- **D.** It's muscle beach party-time for me ☐

You get 10 points for every "C" answer. If your physical score is less than 40, you're in trouble and weight training might save you.

**BUILDING THE
FOUNDATION**

At Home or Abroad

There are advantages to working out at home. You don't have to travel. No one can watch you shower. It's cheaper and it's rarely crowded. On the other hand, it's no fun to be grunting through some grueling bench press sets to find a cocktail party forming around you. And of course, there's always the temptation of game shows and the occasional insect to distract you from your work.

Despite the disadvantages of at home weight training, it's often the most sensible place for the novice kitty lifter. After a few weeks of pumping *chez vous*, you'll be able to show up at the gym with at least muscle nubs, and you won't feel compelled to strip behind a towel.

At Home

You'll need some basic equipment. A manual typewriter makes a good substitute for a Catilus machine. Canned food, especially Italian tomatoes, chunk tuna, and artichoke hearts will serve as weights. Don't forget a mirror. When I'm tossing the tuna at home I find the bathroom with its mirrors and sturdy equipment an ideal spot.

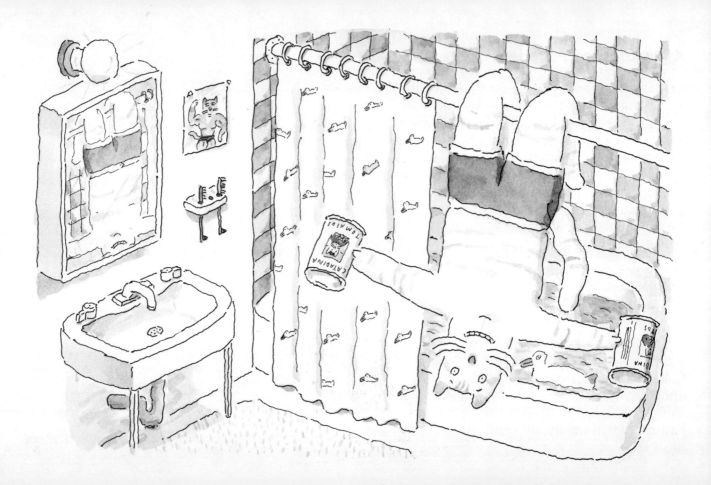

At the Gym

When you find that your own cat sweat is no longer enough, it's time to join a good gym where the heady stimulation of hordes of pumping kitties will drive you to higher achievement. Choose your gym carefully, as it will become your home for your weight-lifting career. Don't frequent a gym that's filled with desperate looking cats or cats who take all their calls at pay phones.

Once you've chosen your gym you'll want to make a good impression. These tricks will help you to pump with panache anywhere:

• Select your gym bag carefully. Avoid designer bags. Cats with initialed bags are called "disco discs" and nobody will whirlpool with them.

• Get a rubber stamp that reads "100 pounds." Use it for stamping empty tuna cans, your gym bag, your bottle of shampoo, your chocolate bars, and your flea collar. This will impress your colleagues and boost your ego.

• Don't try to solve world problems at the gym. The gym is a temple to the body and anybody who starts mouthing off about the Middle East, carcinogens in perfumed litter, or illegal Siamese cat immigrants is out of place. There's only one way to work the jaw muscle at the gym and that's with weights.

• Be patient and considerate. It's not polite upon seeing another kitty pumping only 15 pounds to say, "I pumped 15 pounds before I was weaned," or "Don't bust your flea collar with the strain, buddy."

To Dress or Not To Dress

Give due attention to the proper work-out apparel. Arriving at a steamy gym in a tuxedo will make everyone nervous and if you're mistaken for a penguin, you might be attacked. On the other hand, if you underdress you'll have trouble "psyching" yourself and people might comment on your lack of style.

The Ultimate Drop-Dead Top-of-the-Line Kitty Lifting Costume

Don't mess around with baggy cat shorts. Think of your gym suit as investment dressing and go right to the top of the line. A vibrantly colored lycra spandex catsuit will have tails twitching with envy. Get a color

29

that matches your eyes. If your eyes are different colors you'll be delighted to learn that the latest catsuits come in green/blue, green/gold, etc. Your suit should be form-fitting, but make sure there's enough tail allowance.

You may not want to wear your catsuit for everyday workouts but for competition it's a must. One last word about catsuits: spandex snags. If you're doing kitty lifts with a friend while wearing your catsuit, make sure he's been declawed.

Nude Training

A popular alternative to a catsuit is raw fur. Many kitties prefer to train in the nude. It allows the pores to breathe and saves on hours of post-workout grooming time. I do not, however, recommend nude training at co-ed gyms. Every few years some kitties defy tradition and decency and doff their catsuits in mixed company. While I've never heard of any fatalities, suffice it to say that their weight training suffered as a result.

The Crucial Warm-Up

Always warm up before commencing a training session. "Warming up" doesn't mean lying in the sun for a substantial nap. This is a common misconception. The real point of a warm-up is not to toast the fur but to get the blood moving.

The Curl & Hurl

The favorite and most effective warm-up is called the "curl & hurl." This is easily mastered and is guaranteed to get the blood purring. Here's how: Run as fast as you can down the hall, curl into a furball, and hurl yourself into the bedroom door. Repeat three or four times before beginning a workout. Remember: No pain, no gain!

Here are a few auxiliary warm-ups:
• Climb the living room drapes, tap the ceiling, return to floor. Repeat four times.
• Jump from a second-story window and land on feet three times.
• Pick a fight with a dog.

Warm-ups for Couples

Your warm-up session can be filled with fun if your mate joins you. Here are some warm-ups that are designed with couple cats in mind.

• **The Mate Press.** Kitty A lies on back with all paws in the air. Kitty B sits on the paws of Kitty A. Kitty A alternately flexes and extends legs keeping Kitty B balanced at all times. Obviously this exercise is much more fun for Kitty B but Kitty A will soon have monstrous leg muscles and the unwavering trust and gratitude of Kitty B.

• **The Double Cat Roll.** Kitty A lies on back with paws extended. Kitty B, *facing in the opposite direction,* stands on outstretched paws of mate. Both kitties grasp the tail of their mate in their mouth and begin to roll as one unit. A banked track is recommended.

Concentration

Any two-bit tom can pump up a pec by dancing on the backyard fence. What sets the serious cat in training as a breed apart is the ability to concentrate. Here are three exercises that will sharpen your concentration to pinpoint precision:

- Find a dust mote in the air. Close your eyes halfway and watch it for half an hour.
- Find a chicken bone. Watch it for 15 minutes. Walk away.
- Sit in the sink and watch the faucet drip for half a day.

A Note on Breathing

No matter what anyone's told you in the past, it is absolutely crucial to breathe while exercising. And you've got to breathe both ways: *in* as well as *out*. Some cats get only half the message and *inhale only*. They often wind up floating on the gym ceiling like balloons or even exploding. So don't stint on your breathing. After all, air, even at the gym, is free.

KITTY
NUTRITION:
FOOD FOR
THOUGHT

The body building regime outlined in my book rests squarely on the following great truth: Food is Nice.

Flex's Five Essential Food Groups

If you get a lot of food everyday from each of the five food groups, your body will sprout some fab muscles in no time.

Group A: Italian Food

We just can't thank the Italians enough for their contributions to cat nutrition. Lasagna, spaghetti, pizza, ravioli, manicotti . . . I could go on forever. One of the best features of Italian food is that it's usually a *combination* of foods—like pasta, cheese, and meat or chicken,

cheese, and tomatoes—that acts like a sort of nutritional multi-vitamin for the cat in training. Italian food comes in red and white. You should include four generous helpings a day of selections from the Italian Food Group.

Group B: Bakery Products

Bakery products give energy over the long haul. The wise kitty who stuffs himself with cheese danish and black forest cake will have the stamina to get through every busy demanding kitty day with a minimum of stress to his system.

Bakery products are available in two forms: sweet and bread. I prefer fruit-filled sweet bakery items such as strawberry shortcake and pineapple cheesecake. But most anything that comes in a white bag or neatly tied cardboard box will do the trick. Five helpings per day from the Bakery Group of essential foods is a must.

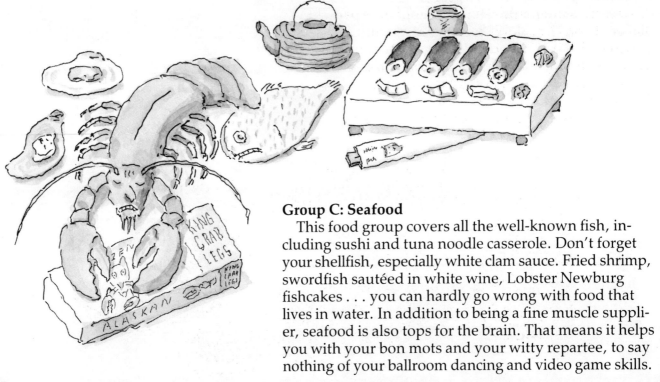

Group C: Seafood

This food group covers all the well-known fish, including sushi and tuna noodle casserole. Don't forget your shellfish, especially white clam sauce. Fried shrimp, swordfish sautéed in white wine, Lobster Newburg fishcakes . . . you can hardly go wrong with food that lives in water. In addition to being a fine muscle supplier, seafood is also tops for the brain. That means it helps you with your bon mots and your witty repartee, to say nothing of your ballroom dancing and video game skills.

Group D: Dessert

Dessert is often mistakenly thought of as part of the Bakery Food Group. When was the last time you saw a Peach Melba or a tapioca pudding at the bakery? You can fill your nutritional requirement for dessert with pistachio ice cream, caramel custard, baked alaska, banana fritters, or strawberry soufflé. Include something from the Dessert Group at least three times a day.

Group E: Hors d'Oeuvres

This is an oft-neglected food group, but it can spell the difference between a merely comely cat and one that's Olympic quality. The Hors d'Oeuvres Group includes nachos, cheese straws, barbequed chicken wings, ham spread, roquefort balls, tiny hot dogs, and the whole world of patés. Have a hefty helping of hors d'oeuvres before every eating experience.

The Perfect Food

CHOCOLATE—the "perfect food" that fills all your nutritional needs, keeps you dancing till dawn, and tastes great. As versatile as it is delicious, chocolate can be ladled over ice cream, eaten with nuts or fruit, baked into cakes, or just eaten as it comes from the package. My favorite chocolate treats include hot fudge sundaes, double chocolate chip ice cream, sacher torte, mocha cream pie, triple fudge brownies, huge slabs of chocolate layer cake, and truffles.

Flex's Daily Dozen (Meals, that is)

I, Flex, have three main principles that guide me in my training diet. I call them my 3 F's. I insist that my meals be:
- FUN
- FILLING
- FREQUENT

Frequent meals are the mainstay of a kitty in training. I try to have a dozen meals a day, jam-packed with as many of the Essential Food Groups as possible. To save confusion I try to include all five groups in every meal.

I eat whenever I'm hungry and out of the twelve waking hours in my days, that happens about once on the hour. Oh, sure, sometimes I deviate from that master plan; no one can be a saint during the holidays. But over the years I've found the Daily Dozen has kept me fit as a fiddle and in fighting trim.

Tips for the Tubby Tabby

Many kitties are initially attracted to weight training because their furry bodies have grown way out of proportion. While weight training is certainly a step in the right direction, the clever fat cat will pay special attention to *all* methods of reduction.

The Hot Fat Principle
of Weight Loss

An overweight kitty, even one who's not going into serious competition, will have little success with weight training. He will be a magnet for ridicule in the locker room. The sight of his reflection in bikini briefs will so depress him that he will forever renounce the sport and make fun of it at cocktail parties in a pathetic effort to save face. This is a shame, especially because it is not at all difficult to melt a fat cat down to size.

Cats have long known that heat melts fat. But few kitties have incorporated this principle into their weight-training program. This is a waste of natural resources and, as solar slenderizing is free, there's no excuse these days for a soft droopy underbelly.

Here are a few Hot Fat reducing methods that I've carefully developed and tested over the years:

• Find a sunny windowsill. Sleep for ten minutes on one side, ten on the other. Stretch and walk stiff-legged in a circle so the fat can run out between your toes.

• Wait until your favorite show is on TV. Climb aboard. Spread your midsection over the top of the tube and snooze. Twitch your tail now and again as the fat drips off it.

• Ride the top of the dryer for ten minutes. You won't be able to sleep but the vibrations are delicious and the rendered fat acts as a fabric softener.

The Truth Behind Water Weight

Just as heat melts fat, so water melts muscle. It is far too complicated to explain how. Suffice it to say that for the cat in training, a bath is a serious setback. And, as if melting muscle weren't bad enough, water will also seep into low-lying regions of your body causing that fluffy bloated look.

Avoid baths at all costs. Become adept with colognes. Rolling on bath mats, you will often pick up a coating of talcum powder that will keep you fresh for days. One of the joys of weight training is that after a few months of serious pumping, no one will dare try to bathe you.

The Flex Super High-Protein Shake

Even the best of cat diets occasionally needs a super power boost to put those muscles over the top. The following recipe is guaranteed to give you a fabulous rush as well as that delicious "full" feeling.

First get out the old blender. Turn it on low and toss in the following items being careful to replace the lid after each addition:
- One Twinkee
- One ounce Rum Raisin ice cream
- Two tablespoons Super Chunky peanut butter

Once this gets to a nice creamy state, turn off the blender and add:
- One half-can fudge frosting
- One cup chocolate chips
- Five ounces catnip

Turn the blender to "pulverize." While it's running toss in:
- A frozen mouse
- One can strawberry tuna, drained and flaked.

Blend for five minutes. Pour and enjoy!

THE
PROGRAM

At last we come to the real heart of cat weight training: The Program. My program has been developed after years of cat competition and reading a few government pamphlets.

The Legs: The Foundation of Cat Body Power

There are two sets of muscles that keep the cat leg on the go: The "rats" to the rear and the "flats" in the foreground. Study these muscles carefully. If you mix them up and do the wrong exercises, you'll find yourself walking backwards.

Here are a few leg exercises:

• **Russian Rounds.** This bulks up those "rats" and is fun to boot. Killer learned it from some weight-lifting cats from Moscow.

Put on some balalaika records.

Stand in a circle with a few friends.

Fold your arms across your chest and kick alternate legs to the center of the circle.

Flats

Rats

Russian Blues love this exercise but they are not necessarily better at it than tabbies.

• **Flying Cat Hops.** This sculpts the rats and flats while it gives impressive spring to the paws.

Stand beneath a hanging bird cage or plant.

Do fifteen standing vertical jumps with a barbell in your mouth.

• **Serious Cat Squat.** This exercise wreaks havoc on the flats and the rats and it's unbeatable for a four-leg frenzy.

Take a relaxed position under a three-inch legged dresser.

Try to stand up.

Repeat ten times.

• **Cat-a-Pult.** This is designed mainly for the flats but it's also a fine total-body conditioner. Don't try this one if you're a beginner: a botched cat-a-pult is a dog's dream.

Stand in place and breathe deeply.

Start running and when you get up some speed fling

yourself into the air aiming at somebody's shoulder, an antique sideboard, or a set of window blinds.

Extend claws on contact.

Slide onto the floor and into your beginning position.

Repeat four times.

Some Practical Applications of More Powerful Cat Legs

As with all the exercises in this book, I urge you to give some thought to the practical applications.

• Builds dazzling speed. This is useful for hiding very quickly. It can spell salvation when the cat-carry case comes out of the closet.

• Builds all-over body power. The "weakest link" concept: If your legs are strong you'll be strong all over. This will allow you to inflict great harm on those who sit in your chair.

• Builds endurance. This is crucial for the modern cat who is often forced to endure bouts with the latest theories on "cat obedience."

• Builds general dance floor skills including waltz, fox trot, disco, and new wave.

• Builds astonishing proficiency at the Limbo and all other popular Caribbean activities that can change your winter vacations forever.

The Chest: The Most Impressive Part of the Well-Honed Cat Physique

The Chest. Yes, the chest: The core of the cat's being, the very essence of metaphysical incandescence, and a good place to pin medals. When completely developed, it is the single most impressive part of the cat physique.

A Note on the Chest and Self-Image

Never become a "mirror athlete." To make a good impression, you must not only have a powerfully developed chest, you must display it tastefully. Wearing a slightly revealing tank top is all right but you should avoid tattooing messages on your chest that say "Built like a Brick" or "I Brake for Persians."

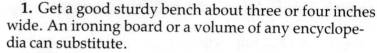

The Bench Press

1. Get a good sturdy bench about three or four inches wide. An ironing board or a volume of any encyclopedia can substitute.

2. Lie down on your back on the bench. If you feel like you're going to fall off, remove your flea collar and use it as a belt attaching yourself to the bench.

3. Have your spotter hand you a heavy bar or a ½ gallon of burgundy. Start from the "down" position and push the bar to arm's length about eight times in succession.

4. Breathe naturally with your mouth open all the time unless you have fish breath which might offend your spotter.

Some Benching Tips for the Novice

• Make sure your paws are clean. Greasy paws have been the downfall of more than one bodybuilder as massive barbells slipped onto their midsection making permanent unsightly dents.

• I have seen cats do a bench press with girlfriends hanging on to the end of the barbells. I've lost all patience with this kind of showing off. If you won't think of yourself, think of the female kitties who could have their tails crushed with an ill-timed slip.

The Pitfall of Chest Training and How to Avoid It

We've all seen cats who've overdone it with the bench press. These kitties can't stand up because their legs can't support the massive weight of their pendulous pecs. They usually wind up in the pound or are sold as bathmats. Don't let it happen to you!

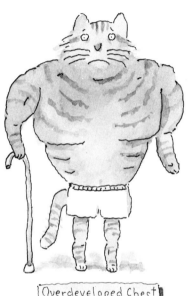

Overdeveloped Chest

The Midsection: That Oft-Neglected Body Part

Most cats have trouble with the elusive midsection right from the beginning. The most common question I get from cats eager to start training is "Midsection: heck, what's that?" The answer is deceptively easy. The midsection is the "rectus abdominis" or, as we call it in the business, the "rabs." The rabs extends from the nose-break to the apostrophe. The most important functions of the rabs are to hold food and to keep the tail out of the ears.

The Three Techniques

Here are three techniques for tummy toughening:

• **Flexing Movements**. The "catroll." It is an all-over body flex that's super for the tummy.

Lie on your back.

Curl your tail forward and catch it in your mouth.

Roll forward and continue rolling for about 300 meters.

The ideal catroll in action looks like a furred hula hoop. It's best to do this on a banked track if possible with no lady cats around as they sometimes get excited and pounce.

• **"Impact" Exercises**. These include all the block and tackle exercises. The cat who is serious about impact work will eventually be able to deflect microwave ovens and typewriters at a distance of 15 feet.

For the beginner, a set of lead mice is the traditional tossed object. Substitutions: a travel alarm or a Hummel figurine.

Lie on the floor on your back and have your spotter, who is about 5 feet above you, toss the object at your midsection. You may want to wear a face mask.

In a few weeks you can move up to small appliances.

• **Hanging Exercises**. Hanging exercises are perfectly safe unless you've been declawed in which case you'll need to buy "grippers" to strap to your front paws.

There are two "hangers": The two-paw and the four-paw. The two-paw is done by hanging on a window drape, chair back or shower curtain by means of the front paws. The four-paw is accomplished by suspending yourself *between* two objects like the front and back car seat or either side of the bathtub in preparation for a bath.

Tails of Titans

Many cats ignore the tail in favor of the "showier" muscle groups such as the chest, legs, and jaws. This is a crippling error as the titanic tail is the mark of the serious muscle cat.

• Enormous tail power will enable you to fell two dogs at your rear while besting another in front.

• Ripping locks off refrigerator doors becomes a piece of catnip.

• With the help of another muscle-tailed cat you can, by standing end-to-end, provide a furry jump rope for your friends.

A Tail of Caution

The tail is fundamentally easy to develop as it responds quickly to exercise. There are, however, certain cautions worth noting. For one thing, one can sometimes *overdevelop* this crucial part. To compound the problem, muscle gained on the tail is not easily lost. Train carefully and *watch those proportions!* Otherwise you risk spending the rest of your lives looking like some wise guy sutured you to a piece of Genoa salami.

Basic Tailwork

OK, we're ready to pump some tail iron!

Here are three basic exercises for the tail musclebound for glory:

• **The Tail Dumbbell Pull**. Hook the tail over a heavy dumbbell. Drag it across the living room floor eight times, rest and repeat. Not only does this build an impressive tail, but incidentally helps to build massive thigh muscles as well. Of course it can be done with a larger barbell but you will totally destroy the living room.

Overdeveloped Tail

64

• **The Two-Cat Isometric Tail Tug-of-War**. This is a very beneficial movement, though it requires the cooperation of another cat or a very weak dog. In this fine movement, the two animals stand rump to rump, wrap tails together and pull in opposite directions.

As the name implies, the stress here is "isometric" rather than "isotonic": that is, very little actual motion of either animal is involved. The static stress on the tail muscles will cause them to increase in size and force.

• **The Double Pulley Tail-O-'Ciser Catilus Progressive Weight Pull**. Hook your tail over the central ring of the Catilus machine, pull the ring down, thus raising the suspended weights upwards, and s-l-o-w-l-y let the weights down again.

DANGERS:

1. The ambitious cat will try to add weight too fast thus winding up as the aforementioned Genoa salami replica.

2. Too much weight can stretch the tail out of shape and the disappointed cat will look like a rope is following him.

JAWS: The Making of
Monster Mouth Muscles

The jaws are the finishing touch on any fabulous feline physique. Well developed jaws lend distinction, nobility, and power to the cat head.

When I was young the most important bodybuilding contest was Mr. Catosphere. It drew the best in the cat body world. It was my first competitive experience, so I worked my legs, my tail, and my midsection until I was in top-notch shape. Kittens quaked when they saw me coming.

My trainer kept encouraging me to work my jaws but I was convinced that it would be a waste of time—after all, I had naturally fine jaws. Well, Mr. Catosphere night arrived and I invited my parents, my wife and our first litter, and the whole neighborhood. It was to be my night of glory. Imagine my horror when, in the first elimination I overhead one judge say to another, "That Flex is a nice piece of catmeat but those jaws are strictly from hunger." Needless to say I disappointed everyone

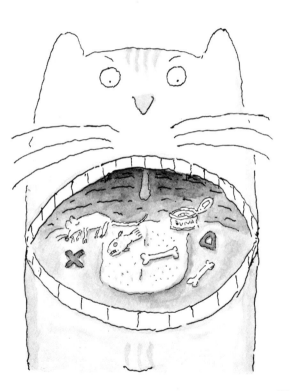

that night and spent weeks slinking around with my tail between my legs.

Now, let's do some mouth work.

• **The Kitty Carry.** This is a good one to do while you watch TV. You will need a 5 lb. dumbbell or a large bag of litter.

Pick up the object in your mouth.

Look to the left and the right as if you were about to steal a chicken bone.

Put your object down.

Repeat twenty times.

• **The Kitty Crunch.** This is the progressive resistance principle in action! Begin crunching frozen cheese blintzes and work your way up to steak bones, sour balls, and frozen mice—always trying to chew as fast as you can.

Items consumed during jaw exercises don't count as far as your diet is concerned.

• **The Mouth Curl.** There's more to the mouth curl than sneering at dried cat food. The mouth curl, one of the best all-around jaw builders, is usually performed

with a Catilus machine. Start with about a 15 lb. weight.

Grasp the bar in your mouth and cha cha for three verses of *Strangers in the Night*.

Tabby Terrific loved this exercise but he would always lose concentration, begin singing and drop the barbell on his feet.

• **The Lamp Hang.** This is good for concentration and all-over toning as well as building a ferocious jaw.

Leap for a hanging lamp or chandelier. (In a pinch you can use the shade of a standing lamp.)

Grasp a lamp part in your teeth and hold that position for fifteen minutes.

Advantages of Highly Developed Jaws

There's nothing like the Jaws of Godzilla to keep your property bird-free. In addition, many cats have found their need for tools diminished by 24 percent after following a jaw exercise program. Even if you never get to the point where you're chewing through salmon cans, you'll still be able to dazzle the ladies with a drop dead smile.

Whisker Workouts: The Finishing Touch for the Highly Advanced Trainee

Whiskers—the quintessential feline facial feature. They play no small role in developing the kitty physique. So don't neglect them.

Whiskers serve as a barometer of overall jaw and facial muscle development. The well-trained kitty should be able to move the whiskers in fairly complicated ways. Inability to do so is a sure sign of poorly developed facial muscles.

Here are a few beneficial whisker exercises:

• **The Semaphore Code**. The idea here is to hang eensy little flags on the whiskers and talk to the cat next door via Semaphore Code. This not only trains the muscles, but gives you a useful skill.

• **The Cocktail Dip**. Lean your face into a plate of cocktail hors d'oeuvres impaling as many olives and anchovies as possible on your whiskers. Eat the tidbits by angling the whiskers forward. Repeat ten times.

As always, use your imagination in developing your own movements. Now some kitties may lack the ability to move the whiskers at all. Killer Kittee had this problem early in his career. It can usually be overcome by more attention to grooming and a gelatin supplement to your diet.

Sex and the Serious Muscle Cat

Many cats who are committed to weight training worry about their sex lives. They wonder if they'll be as potent and as pleasure-prone if they pump iron. The answer is a howling *yes*. In my interviews with muscle cats around the world I've gathered the following statistics:

Sex life	100%
Sex life improved after weight training	86%
Sex life not affected by weight training	12%
Don't know	2%

So you can see, if you're turning-off, don't point at your pecs as the problem. If you're turning on more than you would have believed possible in your pre-weight-training days, welcome to the club!

TO THE LADIES

It used to be that any female kitties caught flexing their flats were considered unfeminine or "doggy." They were warned that their lives would be shortened. Now that we've put a cat on the moon, we certainly should be able to dispel these myths. As a lady, you'll be glad to know your hormones insure that no muscle can get really big. You might have to wear a slightly larger tube top after training but you will never look like a walking basketball collection.

Weight training is, in fact, an excellent activity for the female feline. It can make her sleek and sexy while enabling her to deflect unwanted advances with impunity. It can be especially beneficial if you live in a multi-cat household.

Many ladycats are first attracted to weight training because it's the only way to spend time with their muscle cat mates. They don catsuits and high-tail it to the gym to keep an eye on Mr. Macho Cat. But once they start pressing, a pack of bull terriers couldn't keep them away.

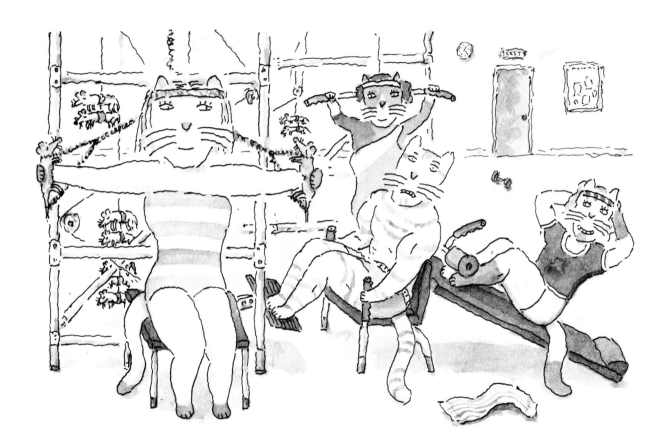

Workout Principles for Ladycats

Fundamentally, lady weight training is not different from male weight training, except the weights are usually pink instead of mouse gray or blue. Of course, you must begin with smaller weights and work up gradually to your 100 pound mouse lobs.

Diet for the Ladycat in Training

Just because you're in training doesn't mean you can neglect your diet and figure that you'll work off those fried tuna balls at the gym. No, the ladycat in training must follow her diet with all the attention she brings to a new Morris movie.

Exercise for the Expectant Mamacat

Should the expectant mamacat indulge in a weight-training program? Though I can't speak from experience I think it makes sense. Otherwise, you could spend too much time napping and not be in prime physical shape for the blessed events. Just be sure to drink lots of milk and cut down on your curl & hurls and your push-ups.

Exercise After That First Litter: Yes or No?

Be reasonable. You can't resume three-hour workouts when you've got a half-dozen kittens mewing for hourly feedings. The first few days of new motherhood are hard enough! Once those little ones are a week old and beginning to explore career opportunities, you can certainly resume a modified workout program.

Exercises Tailored to the Mamacat:

• **The Kitten Curl.**
Lie on your back.
Take four kittens and rest one on each paw.
Relax each leg and then extend them all at once taking care not to drop the little ones.
Repeat ten times.
This exercise strengthens the legs and teaches the kittens respect for their mother.

• The Baby Bounce.

Sit on your haunches holding a kitten in your mouth.

Lower the kitten to the floor while gently stretching your spine.

Return to beginning position.

Repeat eight times.

This stretches and massages your back as it gives you a break from nursing.

• The Broom Boost.

This is another one that gets the kids into the act.

Get a broomstick or your old baton from high school cheerleading days.

Dangle a half dozen or so kittens from the stick.

While resting on your haunches, raise and lower the stick keeping the spine straight and the "flats" firm.

This is great for the pecs and it keeps the kids out of your fur for a while.

BEACH
BLANKET
KITTY

A La Plage or At the Beach

Every cat who's serious about his weight training knows the importance of a high quality tan. A bronzed cat body allows the play of light to highlight rippling kitty muscularity. And if you are interested in competition, an impressive tan is a must. Many muscle cats spend a good part of their life at the beach maintaining that glow that spells "HOT CAT BOD" in bold letters. Life at the beach can be fun. There's surf and tuna sandwiches, volleyball and swimming, not to mention all those foxy ladycats in those tiny bikinis. Unfortunately, many cats think that the beach means "anything goes." This ruins things for the rest of us and gives muscle cats a bad name. Here is some straight talk on beach behavior.

The Best-Loved Beach Work

The best all-around basic beach body toner is jogging. Killer Kittee says the best jogging beach in the world is Waikiki Beach in Hawaii but no matter what beach you jog on, be sure to observe the rules of the road: Pass on

the left, signal when turning, and keep within local speed limits.

Tanning

Tanning. That's the one and only reason for beaches. If tanning weren't so important, God wouldn't have had air and water separated by sand. Now you probably know the basic of tanning that fill the kitty mags: How to put mouse ears over your eyes to prevent burning, how to build up gradually to your proper color, how to wear a caftan like you were born in one, and how to put zinc oxide on your tail. All this is very important. But I have a suggestion that could just make your tan the cat's pajamas. I call it a "Catisserie." It works much like those bird spinners you've seen in deli windows, and it's simple to make:

Catisserie

1. Attach a ½-inch dowel to an old lawn mower motor. You'll need a few of those stretchy things with hooks on the ends that keep luggage on your roof rack. Have a friend help tie them around you and the dowel.

2. Have someone pull the cord on the motor.

That's it! Once that motor's purring, you'll be too.

In a couple of hours you'll be brown as a Burmese. Best of all, there'll be no unsightly white patches on your sides or the insides of your elbows.

NOTE: If you want to get fancy, you can hook up a shower spray device that regularly hits you with a mist of tanning oil.

Kissing, Etc.

Many kitties have asked me about lovemaking on the beach. Fine. OK. *If* you observe a few simple rules. Try for privacy. Otherwise you're liable to ruin volleyball games and frighten kittens. When it comes to noise, less is best. Cats yowling in the heat of passion attract dogs and drown out radio music. Keep it simple. Group activity, chanting, and funny appliances somehow seem unnatural in the fresh air. Finally, stick to the cat you came with.

Showing Off

I hate to make an issue of this but muscle cats can be the biggest show-offs in the world. Really! Now it's easy to see why a formerly flabby kitty would want to strut and flex a bit. But enough's enough.

• Don't pump your pecs when you pull a kite out of the sky.
• Don't rip the sleeves off your T-shirt to show off your biceps.
• Don't grit your teeth and mangle the sandwich baggie. Open the end with the twist tie.
• Don't call your monster muscles into play unless they're needed.

If a kitten is drowning or the lifeguard stand is about to fall over, *that's* your cue. But save it for the real emergencies.

Beach Bullies

There's something about a beach that brings out the bullies. They wait all winter for the chance to get out there and kick sand in somebody's peanut butter. It's a bummer, no doubt about it.

You, as a muscle cat, have to deal with bullies carefully. After all, your body is a lethal weapon. The Mangler just knocks cats unconscious. It works for him. Killer likes to get in some verbal ripostes—a few jokes at the bullies' expense—while he flexes and ripples his monumental muscles. His favorite lines are "Looks like a cat, only dumber" and "Whoa! Tide must be going out around here!"

Practice your own beach-bully tactics at home so you'll be ready when the need arises.

THE
COMPETITIVE
CAT

Advice from the Pros for Cats Musclebound for Glory

Many of you kitties will become such devotees of weight training that you will begin to yearn for some applause. This means you're ready for competition. There are many books available on the fine points of cat competition (see, for example *Musclebound for Mr. Cat America* by Charles Catlas) so I won't go into detail on the basics of the sport. But there are a few things you should know:

• TV appearances are where it's at for the competitive cat. The tube can bring you to the public spotlight, build your fan club, and increase your support at all cat body-building competitions. A guest shot on Johnny Catson brought the Killer three movie offers and 34 marriage proposals.

• Write an autobiography. The Mouse Mangler says that despite his 6 volumes of poetry, he was a virtual unknown at cat competitions. But when his ground-breaking, warts-and-all autobiography, *I, a Cat*, hit the

stands, the Mangler had it made. He won the Mr. Cat Olympia that same year.

• Open a chain of gyms across the country. Not only will cats flock to your spas thus making you a fat cat, *but* you can spot upcoming competitive cat bodybuilding talent and nip it in the bud.

• If you get a guest appearance on a TV sit com, handle it with dignity. When Tabby Terrific did a spot on Love Boat, he tarnished the image of cat bodybuilders everywhere by puncturing an inflatable lifeboat with his claws in a crucial scene. Tisk, tisk, Tabby!

94

Well, muscle cats, now you know everything it takes to build yourself into a paragon of pussy power: the exercise, the diet, the sex tips, the wardrobe. There's just one more crucial component to a cataclysmic catbody: desire. That's right, desire. No cat ever became Mr. Cat Olympia without a fierce, burning desire. A desire stronger than the urge to nap. A desire more powerful than the call of catnip. A desire more insistent than the lure of litter.

Many cats are content to be dilettantes. They'll train for a few weeks and then get distracted by a ball of twine. But the cat with desire perseveres. It was desire that got those cat faces up on Mt. Catmore and desire that got Morris a contract in the high three figures. Desire can build your furry, lumpy cat body into a mound of glistening tanned muscle fiber. Desire can make you the cat you were meant to be. So remember, desire is what gets the tough going when the going gets tough.

That's it, you crazy cats. Now get out there and lift something.

A FINAL WORD

About The Author

Anthony Serafini is a philosophy professor, a former weight-lifter, and author of THE MUSCLE BOOK. He lives with his kitty, FLEX THE CAT, and his wife in Massachusetts.

About The Artist

Paul Meisel is an artist who lives and works in New York City. His work has appeared in *The New York Times*, *Book Digest*, and other publications. WEIGHT TRAINING FOR CATS is his first book project.